AGILE SOFTWARE TESTING

The Agile Software Testing course covers the methodologies and testing approaches but also the techniques and tools used in software testing in agile projects.

The first section of this course is on Methodologies and Testing Approaches.

Agile software development lifecycles are comprised of short iterations with working software released at the end of each iteration.

In this section, you will have overview of agile development and cover some of the different approaches, including Extreme Programming, Scrum, and Kanban.

You will learn the key aspects of testing in an agile environment, as well as the skillset that an agile tester should have.

More specifically we are going to cover the following:

- *Agile Software Development Fundamentals* which includes Agile Software Development and the Agile Manifesto, The Twelve Principles of the Agile Manifesto, The Whole Team Approach, Early and Frequent Feedback;

- *Aspects of Agile Approach* which includes Extreme Programming (XP), Scrum, Kanban, Collaborative User Stories, Creation of User Stories, Retrospectives, Continuous Integration, Release and Iteration Planning;

- *Testing in Agile Approaches* which includes Agile Testing and Development Activities, Agile Project Work Products, Agile Test Levels, Agile Testing and Configuration Management, Agile and Independent Testing;

- *Test Status in Agile Projects* which includes Communicating Test Status and Product Quality, Managing Risk Regression;

- *Role and Skills of an Agile Tester* which includes Skills of an Agile Tester, Role of an Agile Tester.

The second section of this course is on Techniques and Tools.

Agile approaches include the complementary techniques of test-driven development, acceptance test- driven development, and behavior-driven development

In this section, we will explore the key features of agile testing and how techniques such as black box testing can be applied in agile projects.

We will also take a look at various tools that are available to agile testers, everything from task management and tracking tools, to communication and configuration tools.

More specifically we are going to cover the following:

- *Agile Testing and Risk Assessment* which includes Test-driven and Behavior-driven Development, Test Levels, A Scrum Tester, Quality Risks in Agile Projects;

- *Techniques in Agile Projects* which includes Estimation of Testing Effort, Test Basis in Agile Projects, Definition of Done, Acceptance Test-driven Development, Functional and Nonfunctional Black Box Test Design, Exploratory Testing;

- *Tools for Testing in Agile Projects* which includes Task Management and Tracking Tools, Communication and Information-sharing Tools, Test Development and Configuration Tools.

METHODOLOGIES AND TESTING APPROACHES

The Agile Software Testing - Methodologies and Testing Approaches is the first part of the Agile Software Testing course.

Agile software development lifecycles are comprised of short iterations with working software released at the end of each iteration.

In this section, you will have overview of agile development and cover some of the different approaches, including Extreme Programming, Scrum, and Kanban.

You will learn the key aspects of testing in an agile environment, as well as the skillset that an agile tester should have.

- *Agile Software Development Fundamentals*: Agile Software Development and the Agile Manifesto, The Twelve Principles of the Agile Manifesto, The Whole Team Approach, Early and Frequent Feedback;

- *Aspects of Agile Approaches*: Extreme Programming (XP), Scrum, Kanban, Collaborative User Stories, Creation of User Stories, Retrospectives, Continuous Integration, Release and Iteration Planning;

- *Testing in Agile Approaches*: Agile Testing and Development Activities, Agile Project Work Products, Agile Test Levels, Agile Testing and Configuration Management, Agile and Independent Testing;

- *Test Status in Agile Projects*: Communicating Test Status and Product Quality, Managing Risk Regression;

- *Role and Skills of an Agile Tester*: Skills of an Agile Tester, Role of an Agile Tester.

AGILE SOFTWARE DEVELOPMENT AND THE AGILE MANIFESTO

After completing this topic, you should be able to recall the statements of value expressed in the Agile Manifesto, on which the principles of agile software development are founded.

Welcome to Agile Software Development and the Agile Manifesto.

In this course, we'll be talking about the history of the Agile Manifesto and we'll also dive into the main values of the manifesto.

The Agile Manifesto was written in February of 2001 by a group of 17 software practitioners of several programming methodologies.

This group went on to create what is now known as the Agile Alliance.

These practitioners had come together to evaluate the ways in which companies and teams doing software development were working together and to discuss better ways of working together.

As a result of coming together, these practitioners came up with and agreed on four main values and 12 principles that embody the spirit of what any Agile framework or methodology is based on.

The Agile Manifesto with its main values forms an umbrella over a number of different Agile methods and frameworks; meaning, that the specifics of implementing some frameworks may be different, but they all share the main values and principles.

The first value that is in the Agile Manifesto states that we value individuals and interactions over processes and tools.

One thing to note as we go through each of these values is that the practitioners that wrote the values claimed that we value the items on the right, but we value the items on the left more.

So, when we say individuals and interactions over processes and tools, that does not mean that we don't value processes and tools, but it means that we value individuals and interactions more than processes and tools.

Also, what that means is that we want to start with people.

Once we figure out people, and the people dynamics, and the interactions that are appropriate, then we can figure out the right processes and tools and those follow after we figured out the first part.

We also want to allow individuals to contribute to the development of a project whether that's in terms of the requirements or improving the way that we do things, improving the way that we work together.

Individuals have great ideas and following processes rigidly does not allow for the contribution of those ideas and of those improved processes.

Another point is with human interaction, we want to readily be able to adapt to new ideas and innovations.

So, we want to create the human interactions in our teams that allow for those that adaptation and that allow for our evolution of new ideas and innovations to fulfil the requirements that we've received.

The second value in the Agile Manifesto states that we value working software over comprehensive documentation.

Many teams spend a lot of time doing comprehensive documentation and writing pages and pages of requirements and spec talks, whereas within Agile methods, we value more reaching to a point where we have working software.

What we mean by working software is that it's been developed, tested, integrated, and documented.

So, as we've noted before, documentation is still important, but we want to achieve the level of documentation that's just enough versus going overboard.

Some of the documentation that you may see in an Agile project will be requirements documentation usually in the form of user stories and acceptance criteria and some of the product technical specifications.

Sometimes, many developers in an Agile framework will document their code within the code itself.

The third value of the Agile Manifesto states that we value customer collaboration over contract negotiation.

What that means is that we really value collaboration over confrontation, over changes and requirements, or adding new things to our original requirements.

We want to feel that we're collaborating with our customers versus negotiating with them.

By collaborating, we're producing better products and we're fulfilling their needs.

The key points when it comes to a customer collaboration that we want to think about are the project start.

So, when do we start the project, the scope, and the time that we expect to spend on the project, and when is the project suppose to end.

Those are usually the main points of collaboration that we want to start looking at in terms of a collaborative mindset versus negotiating.

The fourth and last value of the Agile Manifesto states that we value responding to change over following a plan.

We have to realize that change can be of value and can bring added value to our projects.

We want to be able to respond quickly to that change in order to fulfill our customer's desires and needs also our product users, so the users of the product may be different than the customers who are paying for the products and then also in order to stay ahead of the market.

THE TWELVE PRINCIPLES OF THE AGILE MANIFESTO

After completing this topic, you should be able to outline the twelve principles of the Agile Manifesto, on which agile software development is based.

In this course, we'll be presenting the twelve principles of the Agile Manifesto.

And we'll be talking about them in the order of who is the most impacted by those principles.

There are number of principles in the Agile Manifesto that impacts the customer and that are customer focused.

For example, early and continuous delivery of software, the authors of the Agile Manifesto stated that their highest priority was to satisfy the customer through early and continuous delivery of valuable software, again talking about the importance of delivering value.

Second is welcoming changing requirements. Again, the authors of the manifesto wanted to make sure that teams understood that it's important to welcome changing requirements even in the development phase.

Agile processes harness change for the customer's competitive advantage.

And the only way to do so in many cases is to be flexible when it comes to requirements.

And third deliver working software frequently, some of the iterations can be anywhere between one week and four weeks, but as we have mentioned in other lectures, the preference is to keep the iteration length short.

The Agile Manifesto also has a number of team-focused principles, for example, business and developers work together daily.

The Agile Manifesto emphasizes the importance of the business and the development teams working together daily to produce the best possible outcomes.

Also, build projects around motivated individuals, give people the environment and the support that they need in order to be motivated and trust them to get the job done.

This is a very different mindset than a command and control mindset, where some people in the organization may be acting more as task managers.

And then lastly, emphasis on face to face conversation give people the ability to have face to face communication and conversation and encourage them to do so.

One of the constructs of some of the Agile methods that allows for this, for example, is the daily standup meeting.

By having a daily meeting, where people come together, we're having a lot of verbal communication and face to face communication versus relying only on e-mail.

Some of the development-focused principles are: working software shows progress.

Again, the work...the primary measure of progress in Agile is working software versus documentation or any other measure. Also, sustainable development pace, it's important to maintain a development pace that's sustainable for the team and that doesn't burn people out.

Lastly, requires technical excellence and good design, so Agile methods also wanted to emphasize that it's important to have technical excellence and good design in order to achieve a high quality, high-level product.

The remaining principles in the Agile Manifesto are simplicity and that means simplicity in design, and implementation, and communication and processes.

Self-organizing teams, where people are given the autonomy to figure certain things out like who is working on what tasks.

And then finally, regular team retrospectives and adaptation, when you give people an opportunity to retrospect and adapt their processes on a regular basis, you start to see improvements in processes and improvements in motivation and the way that people work together.

THE WHOLE TEAM APPROACH

After completing this topic, you should be able to describe the whole team approach promoted by agile software development.

In this section, we'll be talking about "the whole team approach", which is a software development approach that was initially presented by extreme programming.

The whole team approach is a collaborative approach to software development that emphasizes the participation of the whole team including business people, designers, developers, testers, et cetera in developing the software that we're producing.

The whole team approach focuses on having smaller teams that typically don't exceed seven members.

The teams between five and nine members were able to have more effective communications than teams that grow beyond that number.

We also focused on having collocated teams or teams that are all seated in the same location.

Having collocated teams removes any barriers between the team members and enables better communication.

The benefits of utilizing a whole team approach are having strong working relationships between team members.

We see more effective cooperation, collaboration, teamwork, and communication. We also see shared knowledge amongst the team.

So instead of one person having all the knowledge around one area of a project, we start to see people sharing their knowledge and more people becoming experts in more areas.

And then finally, everyone collectively is responsible for the outcome of a project.

One aspect of the whole team approach is that everybody is responsible for the quality of the end product.

In order to have that responsibility to be shared, we need to have the support of both developers and testers in producing some of the things that allow us to have higher quality products, such as acceptance tests, test strategies, and automated test suite.

In order to have effective test suites and acceptance tests, we need to make sure that there is a strong communication and collaboration between developers and testers to produce these in the best way possible.

We also encourage having informal meetings where developers and testers might come together to think about the quality of the products and potentially create new product increments based on their discussions.

And then finally, collaboration helps us finalize the feature set and ensure that we have achieved the development and the testing required to have quality products that can be produced and then released into production.

EARLY AND FREQUENT FEEDBACK

After completing this topic, you should be able to recall how the agile software development model incorporates early and frequent feedback.

In this section, we'll be talking about early and frequent feedback and the importance of obtaining early and frequent feedback for agile teams and the mechanisms that allow us to do so.

Early and frequent feedback is vital for agile development teams.

It's a way for us to ensure that the team is headed in the proper direction at every point along the way in developing or completing a project versus waiting until the end.

One of the mechanism or constructs of agile that allows us to obtain early and frequent feedback is the fact that we develop product increments at the end of every sprint.

With each product increment, we have an opportunity to get stakeholder's feedback.

The product backlog that we have created at the beginning of the project and that evolves throughout the life cycle of a project is the blueprint for our product increments.

If you recall, we have spoken about Waterfall development and how Waterfall breaks activities into phases, with each phase being distinctly separated from the next.

So, one of the phases would be design, which then moves us on to development, which then moves us onto testing.

On the other hand, agile development breaks activities into small chunks that we complete in every iteration in order to produce that product increments.

So, feedback is then gathered at the end of each iteration and this is a vital part again of our early and frequent feedback.

That feedback is important for adopting modifications or changes needed to the product, and it helps us deliver the highest business value features for our customers and stakeholders.

The benefits of obtaining early and frequent feedback through the product's increments is that we're able to break down all the requirements so when we create our product backlog, we take the general overall requirements for a project and break them down into smaller chunks and smaller pieces that we can create product increments from.

This helps us avoid mistakes when we approach the project as a larger overall project.

It also helps us achieve robust product development, where we're building exactly what the customer wants by getting the customer's feedback every step along the way.

It also helps us achieve early clarification of customer needs so as the customer is looking through our product increments, testing them, using them, they are able to give us feedback on what's working, what's not working, and what other needs they may have. It also helps reduce misunderstandings of requirements since customers are actually getting their hands on the finalized products increments versus waiting until the end when everything has been integrated.

And finally, early and frequent feedback through product increments helps us achieve continuous improvement by continuing to inspect each product increment, adapt, and improve, and also improve the way that we work together to produce those product increments.

EXTREME PROGRAMMING (XP)

After completing this topic, you should be able to recall the basic features of the Extreme Programming, or XP agile approach.

In this section, we'll be talking about Extreme Programming, or XP, and the main principles and values behind XP. XP is a popular agile methodology that focuses on the ongoing, rapid delivery of small releases of software.

XP relies on close collaboration between team members and the continuous refinement of program requirements through that close collaboration.

XP focuses on having small programming teams that can design, develop, test, and update code, all within the same team.

The core values of Extreme Programming are the following.

Communication, there is a strong focus on positive communication within Extreme Programming teams.

When XP first came out, it was an attempt at coming out of some of the more corporate ways of managing projects and working together as teams, and they wanted to emphasize a strong positive communication between both stakeholders and team members and the team members themselves.

The idea is that with strong collaboration and positive communication, we can get at the best solutions for problems instead of laying blame and pointing fingers.

The next value is simplicity. And simplicity applies to both the technology and the techniques with which we implement technology.

So XP has a strong focus on simple design and simple fulfillment of requirements. One of the next values is feedback.

So XP was one of the first methods or frameworks to incorporate continuous feedback through code reviews between the team members, and peer reviews, as well as stakeholder reviews and demos. And then finally, courage.

So in XP, the value of courage was brought up as a value that the team members should care about, and it's an important one.

We want to have the courage to discard old code when we have better code that we could write or when we have a better or a simpler way of approaching our requirement.

This value helps us let go of certain ideas around possessiveness of code, and it actually opens up the code to be more collaborative amongst team members.

The primary principles of XP are collective ownership.

So, in XP, all developers are responsible for the full body of code including code that they didn't personally work on.

So, if a developer was in the code base and could see some code that needed fixing, their responsibility is to go in and fix it even if that code wasn't theirs or they didn't write it.

Collective ownership encourages collaboration and open communication between team members and helps us elevate the quality of our code.

Next is continuous integration. In continuous integration, code is integrated and tested into the full code base on a regular basis.

So, the entire system is built and tested at least once a day.

Next is energized work. One of the primary principles of XP is that overworked and fatigued team members are more prone to making mistakes, and so we want to create a sustainable pace for team members so that they are constantly energized, more alert, and more productive.

This reduces the number of bugs and issues in our code.

Also having a shared workspace, so teams that are collocated and work together in the same workspace have an opportunity for instant feedback between each other as well as improved communication, and they get a boost of productivity.

And then finally, on-site customer, and what this principle means is that by having access to someone who is either the customer or the customer representative directly on on-site, we can develop our software faster, and we have instant access to that person who is actually defining the requirements that the software must meet.

They are going to be there and available to answer questions immediately versus having long turnaround times.

SCRUM

After completing this topic, you should be able to recall the basic features of the Scrum agile approach.

In this section, we'll be talking about the Scrum Agile framework and about the main concepts behind this framework.

Scrum is an Agile framework that allows us to do software product development with quick iteration cycles.

The focus in Scrum is on producing working product increment after every iteration, which goes back to one of the Agile values and principles where software and working software are the primary measure of progress.

Scrum is based on an iterative approach to the software development cycle.

So, what these means is that projects are broken up into development units called sprints.

A sprint is a time-boxed iteration of the complete software development cycle.

In other words, we do all of the activities involved in a software development cycle and each of those iterations are sprints.

So, in sprints...and in each sprint, we're doing planning and analysis, design and development, testing, and then delivery of the product increment to the customer.

The difference between Scrum and, for example, Waterfall is that in Scrum many of these activities are happening synchronously, so team members are collaborating and working together to do testing alongside development and planning alongside the testing et cetera versus waiting for each phase to complete before moving on to the next phase.

With product increments, we're attempting to deliver potentially shippable software.

What this means is that each product increment contains the highest priority functionality and it should be gone through the whole development cycle, where we have developed it, there has been development testing, there has been testing from the QA team et cetera.

Product increments then grow in functionality with each completed sprint, so we may start with a minimal implementation of a feature or functionality that then grows more robust as we go on to the next sprints.

There are number of core roles within Scrum. Those three core roles are the product owner, the team, and the Scrum master.

The product owner is really responsible for the product's backlog, creating it, maintaining it, prioritizing it, and decisions regarding what is important and not important for the team to focus on.

The product owner also accepts or rejects each product increment that the team delivers.

The team is responsible for figuring out how to produce what the product owner needs; how to collaborate who does what and be a self-organizing team that autonomously reaches and fulfills their commitment to the product owner.

The Scrum master is the keeper of the process and will stay on top of the process and work with the team to make sure that the right meetings are happening, the right conversations are happening, and the things don't get derailed unnecessarily by others.

KANBAN

After completing this topic, you should be able to recall the Kanban management approach that can be incorporated into agile projects.

In this section we'll be talking about Kanban as an Agile approach for software development.

One of the main characteristics of Kanban is its flexibility, where Kanban mainly focuses on achieving flow for a team by limiting work in progress and redefine work in progress as any active tasks that are currently being worked on.

By limiting the number of tasks that anybody or a team can work on at any given time, we see that teams will collaborate to move things from "In Progress" to "Done" and allows the team to achieve a state of flow, where things are moving and getting done before picking up new work.

In Kanban, the product owner can reprioritize work, where changes outside the current work items don't really impact the team.

One of the most important things is that the product owner ensures that the most important work remains on the top of the backlog.

That way the team is always share that they are working on the maximum value items and delivering those back to the business.

In this scenario, we find that there is no need for iterations of fixed length as long as the team is achieving a state of flow and working through and getting things done based on the highest priority.

One of the main things to calculate or to track in Kanban is cycle time.

Cycle time is a key metric that calculates the amount of time for any unit of work to cycle through the team's workflow.

By understanding our team cycle time, we're able to forecast the delivery of future work.

In order to ensure smaller cycle times, we overlap skill sets on our team, so we have different people that are able to do many different things versus having a single person that holds on to a specific skill sets.

Having single people be responsible for a single type of work can create bottlenecks in a team that's trying to do a Kanban or implement a Kanban framework.

Having overlapping skill sets also allows us to spread knowledge through code review and mentoring.

And those two activities can help us spread knowledge and ensure that we have a cross-functional team.

One of the great things about Kanban is that it helps us achieve efficiency.

By limiting work in progress, we avoid multitasking, which always negatively impacts efficiency.

The key to limiting work in progress is that, work in progress limits help us reveal bottlenecks.

If things are getting stuck In Progress, for example, we're able to see why things aren't moving into Done or we can start investigating why things gets stuck in that state. We're also able to see the causes of why things get stuck.

For example, is there a lack of focus, is it a people issue, is it a skill set issue that we need to enhance on our team?

One other key principle in Kanban is continuous improvements, which is a shared principle across all other Agile frameworks as well.

By having a visual representation of our workflow, which is very typical with teams that are implementing Kanban, we're able to identify bottlenecks and visually, quickly see what the status is of our work items and items that are In Progress.

Some of the charts that we might use in Kanban are called Control charts that help us see the cycle time for each issue or each item that's going through our workflow.

Another chart that we might use is cumulative flow diagrams, which show the number of issues in each state of our workflow.

COLLABORATIVE USER STORIES

After completing this topic, you should be able to describe how collaborative user stories are created to capture requirements in agile projects.

In this section, we'll be talking about the concept of user stories and how they are used and created collaboratively in Agile projects to capture requirements and develop products.

Although, they are not the only way to capture requirements, user stories have become very popular in Agile projects and within Agile teams.

There are number of features and characteristics that user stories have that made them this popular including, user stories are the primary artifacts of development, this means that user stories contain enough information to ensure that the development team knows how to fulfill the requirements.

And if not, it contains enough information to provide a point of conversation.

User stories should also express a discrete functionality that a system must provide.

User stories are used throughout the development process from capturing the initial requirement to including details that come out of conversations with the product's owner and the team to the acceptance criteria necessary to validate that the story fulfills the customer's requirements.

User stories are also realistic and easy for both the team members and customers to understand and they are written in such a way that they can be translated easily into a business requirement as well as a technical requirement.

Also, user stories must be estimable so developers must be able to look at a user story, read it, and understand enough to be able to estimate how long they'll take to implement it.

The components of user stories are a user story is a written description of a required functionality.

And what these means is that the customer or the customer representative, so the product's owner, will produce a written description of something that a system must do or that a user must be able to do with our system.

User stories also contain conversations about the stories.

So when conversations occur between the customer or the customer representative and developers, throughout the release and iteration planning cycles, developers and the product's owner will note those conversations and the results of those conversations in the user stories.

User stories also contain testing requirements or acceptance criteria, which allow the test team to create their test cases.

So, by testing these acceptance criteria, we're able to verify that the customer's needs are being met.

The process of using user stories through planned a development projects can be broken into five main steps as we're going to show in the next.

However, sometimes the order of these steps isn't as important as you see or it's not important to follow the same order that you see.

So obviously, one of the first steps is to write the user stories.

Sometimes, we select an iteration length next or we might select an iteration length with our team that we have stayed consistent with for a long time and that's just the iteration length that we'll use regardless of the user stories that we have just written.

Step 3 is to estimate the work. So, once we look at the user stories, we understand them, we have the right conversations, we're able to then as a team estimate the amount of work required in order to get it done.

Usually, again, in Agile projects, we're estimating by relative estimation, so we're looking at the size and complexity of a story as compared to others. In Step 4, we're prioritizing and allocating stories to either a sprint or a release.

And in Step 5, we're updating estimates and iterations, and this is something that happens at the end of each sprint and sometimes during a sprint as part of our backlog grooming process or at the end of a release.

CREATION OF USER STORIES

After completing this topic, you should be able to describe the techniques for collaborative creation of user stories, such as INVEST, and describe the components of a user story

In this section, we're going to be talking about creating user stories and what to take into consideration when creating good user stories.

We've talked about the process of creating collaborative user stories and the importance that user stories have in the development process for software projects.

In this section, we'll be focusing more on what things to take into consideration in order to ensure that our user stories are good user stories. In order to do so, we have a criteria called invest.

Invest stands for independent, negotiable, valuable, estimable, small, and testable.

And in the next s, we'll be going through each one of these.

So good user stories are independent, which means the stories can be worked on in any order, and this allows for true prioritization.

Technically speaking, sometimes we do have to order certain stories that come before others, but for the most part, we want to reduce any dependencies inbetween stories.

Next is negotiable. When we talk about negotiable user stories, we want to be able to have the opportunity to negotiate some of the terms of user stories with the customer or even with other developers and the testers.

What this means is that user stories should come as a functional requirement or a need that the user has and not a specific way of implementing that need.

This gives the developers and the team the freedom to look into different ways of implementing the requirement and fulfilling the need.

Next is valuable. User stories must deliver value to the end user, and this is one of the main criteria of good user stories.

The value is seen as a project-related value. And with the focus of agile frameworks on delivering higher business value first, then we understand the importance of this criteria for user stories.

Next is estimable. If a user story is too vague, or not specific enough, or too large, it's very hard for team members to estimate the effort required in implementing it.

Therefore, one of the important criteria for good user stories is that they are clear enough and of a size that a team member can quickly identify the relative complexity of that user story.

[Heading: Creation of User Stories. User stories must be estimable to properly prioritize stories based on the effort required to work on it.]

Talking about size, one of the criteria of good user stories is that they are small.

No user stories should require more than a sprint to work on, and we prefer that user stories are actually small enough to complete within one to two days.

By keeping user stories small, we're able to ensure that the user stories we've selected can be developed, and implemented, and tested within the course of a sprint.

And finally, testable. In order to have good user stories, they must be testable, and that requires that we have good acceptance criteria included in the user story.

User stories must be tested fully in order for us to deliver the complete product. So, this is one other very important criteria for good user stories.

RETROSPECTIVES

After completing this topic, you should be able to recall the role of retrospectives in an agile project and describe the role of testers within retrospectives.

In this section, we'll be talking about retrospectives and how they are used by agile teams as an opportunity to improve.

Agile retrospectives are a powerful tool when used by agile teams.

They are special meetings that take place at the end of a specific period of work, usually at the end of a sprint, or iteration, or at the end of a release.

When they come at the end of a sprint, they usually come on the last day of a sprint.

Agile retrospectives should be team-driven, meaning they are focused on issues and things that the team wants to discuss together.

And they are driven by the members of the team versus having somebody be in control of the meeting.

A facilitator is usually required just in order to make sure that the discussions are happening, and everybody has an opportunity to contribute.

The purpose of agile retrospectives is to provide an opportunity for us to inspect and then adapt our processes.

If there are certain processes that we've been implementing that haven't been effective, this is our chance to take a look at those and see how we can improve them.

It also gives us an opportunity to analyze our results.

Are we delivering the quality that we expect to be delivering within our sprints?

Are we delivering at the velocity that we were expecting to be delivering?

And then finally, we're able to identify ways to improve after we've looked at our results and looked at our processes.

Some of the things that we may try to improve as a result of looking and then inspecting our processes within retrospectives are our effectiveness as a team.

Are we building the right things? Are we delivering according to our customers' expectations and are we fulfilling their needs?

Productivity is another one. Are we as productive as we would like to be?

Are we, for example, wasting time on certain processes or other things that we could be instead spending time doing work?

Are we overbooking and trying to do too much within a sprint?

We also might try to improve the quality of our output, either additional exercises or things that we can be implementing within a sprint in order to ensure that our quality is higher.

And finally, satisfaction. Are we satisfied as a team with the environment, with our dynamic?

Are our customers satisfied with our work products?

We also have an opportunity in our retrospective to review the project status.

However, we're going a little bit further than where we went when we were in our review meeting or our demo.

In the demo or the review meeting, we look at which stories were completed, and which stories weren't completed.

And in the retrospective, we can start to look at root causes and why or why not certain stories were completed.

Some of the considerations when planning and implementing agile retrospectives are...to the extent possible, retrospectives should be unique.

It's easy to get into a rut and continue to talk about what went well, what didn't go well, and how can we improve.

A good facilitator will research different ways to facilitate this meeting and make them unique, and exciting, and interesting.

Keep the focus in retrospectives on the current activity.

So, we will keep the focus on the current sprint versus looking too far into the past or looking too far into the future.

Having a retrospective without gathering data upfront is not very useful because data will help the team sort through issues where we can look at root causes and look at things that may have caused some of the results that we're seeing.

Also, we try to encourage as much participation as possible by selecting activities that promote team brainstorming, team learning, and team decision making.

Some other considerations are that retrospectives should not be used for individual performance feedback.

We're looking at our performance together as a team.

While analyzing processes, we're looking at things that went well; we're looking at things that need to be improved at a team level. Individual performance should be handled by managers directly with their reports.

Also talking about our issues in retrospectives is not a solution for inadequate skills on the team.

If we have issues with technical skills or issues collaborating together, those go beyond the scope of a retrospective and should be handled elsewhere.

And then finally, retrospectives are not used to correct the organizational approach to building software.

If an organization has a certain mental model of how software is developed or how teams must work together, retrospectives aren't the right place to fix that.

Again, retrospectives are a very powerful tool that agile teams can use in order to improve, inspect, and adapt.

CONTINUOUS INTEGRATION

After completing this topic, you should be able to recall how continuous integration is implemented in an agile project, describe how testing occurs in this framework, and describe its benefits and challenges.

In this section, we'll be talking about continuous integration as a practice in Agile projects, how continuous integration provides a baseline for testing, and some of the challenges and benefits.

Continuous integration is the practice of merging all developers working copies of code into a mainline branch.

Then we build that merged code at least once a day.

The objectives of continuous integration are to minimize the efforts and overall duration required for each integration.

So by integrating multiple times, then integration stops becoming such a big production and we have less issues to deal with when we do integrate, or handling the issues becomes a lot easier because the change from the last integration to the next one is a smaller change than when we have a large integrations.

Also, one of the objectives is to deliver product versions that are suitable for release, but also that are suitable for testing on an integration testing level.

Continuous integration involves the effective use of Continuous integration servers, which allow us to configure certain times of day when we integrate code, version control tools, which ensure that our code base is version controlled, build tools, unit testing frameworks, and other tools.

So, for example, one of the tools used a lot in continuous integration is Concurrent Versions System, or CVS, some other tools are Ant, MSBuild, JUnit, and others.

Some of the considerations when doing continuous integration are that continuous integration as we have mentioned does rely on having multiple tools integrated and working well together for testing, automation, and version control.

Ensuring that those tools work well together takes time and also some cycles from the development team, but it ultimately pays off in the end.

There also may be scheduling challenges if people are merging in code at the same time or trying to merge in code at the same time that affects each other's code.

It may also seem expensive to do continuous integration with all of the tools and time required. However, the payoff in the end is a lot larger than the cost.

Some of the benefits of continuous integration are that we're able to detect defects early.

It also helps us simplify the debugging process because the difference between the last version of the code and the current version is a small difference.

It also helps us minimize the integration phase when we're integrating code. It provides immediate feedback to developers.

And it raises visibility of a project by making it clearly visible whether the build has worked or whether it has failed.

RELEASE AND ITERATION PLANNING

After completing this topic, you should be able to recall the agile concepts of release and iteration planning.

In this section, we'll be talking about release and iteration planning as activities in Agile projects, and we'll highlight the involvement of testers in these activities.

Release planning is a process that helps teams to find their strategy for implementing a project.

When we do release planning, we set a release goal and a timeframe for the release and then we start thinking about how to split up the work into different iterations.

In the release planning meeting, we're talking at a high level of the functionality required by the system and some of the user stories that will fulfill the requirements of the system.

Testers must be involved in the release planning activity since testers help develop user stories.

They help seek further clarification on user stories by highlighting where there is insufficient information, and they provide some high-level test planning as well as they highlight some testing risks.

Testers have a unique perspective when looking at user stories because they are able to see where the areas that need to be tested are and they are able to see what questions the user stories aren't really answering for purposes of testing.

Iteration planning is an activity that's performed after release planning and it takes some of the user stories and some of the work that's been designated for the next iteration and helps define independent tasks so the team works together to split up the user stories into independent tasks including testing tasks.

During iteration planning, we can do a risk assessment of certain stories, which involves also the testers from a risk perspective.

The tester involvement in iteration planning is to help create acceptance tests for the user stories and to estimate their testing tasks. Iteration planning and release planning are two great opportunities for testers to become involved in the planning process for Agile projects and provide their unique perspective on what clarification is needed in order for testing to go well.

[Heading: Release and Iteration Planning. Information about Iteration planning contains a flow chart with the following steps: Determine target velocity, Adjust priorities, Identify iteration goal, Select user stories, Split user stories into tasks, and Eliminate tasks.

The steps Determine target velocity and Adjust priorities are grouped together under the following heading: Do in any sequence.]

AGILE TESTING AND DEVELOPMENT ACTIVITIES

After completing this topic, you should be able to compare testing and development activities in traditional and agile approaches.

In this section, we'll talk about the role of testing and the inter-action between testing and development in agile projects.

Agile testing is a software testing practice that's different than software testing in traditional waterfall projects.

The difference lies in the fact that agile testing happens alongside development throughout the whole project.

In waterfall projects, testing usually comes at the end of a project after all of the design and development has happened.

In agile projects, testers have a larger role and are involved in the very beginning phases of a project throughout to the delivery of the product.

The advantages of agile testing and the agile testing approach are that it saves time and money.

By involving testers from the very beginning and having them test along the way, we're able to catch bugs when they are smaller or they involve less code, and they have less repercussions than catching issues at the end of a project.

Agile testing also requires less documentation. For the most part, many of the test cases come directly from acceptance criteria that are included in user stories.

Agile testing also ensures that we gather regular feedback by providing feedback from a testing perspective after every sprint or during every sprint.

And agile testing helps us identify issues in advance by being involved even in the planning stages before execution and before development.

So, testers are able to provide feedback on potential issues as well as issues that occur during the course of a sprint.

The phases of testing are aligned with the phases of development. So, for example, in the initiation phase when we're establishing the project's foundation, agile testers are still involved.

They are involved in thinking through the user stories. They are involved in thinking through acceptance criteria and certain risks when it comes to the project.

Next in the construction phase is when development is occurring for the agile project.

Throughout the course of the construction phase, agile testing is an activity that's performed within each sprint and at the end of each sprint.

It's a continuous activity that's performed side by side with development.

The end game is where we transition into production.

So, we take the code that we've developed throughout the construction phase, and we release it to a production environment where users can actually use our code.

In this phase, agile testing is still involved since we may do production testing or a post-release testing.

And then finally, once we're already in production, we may have agile testers involved in showing that the system is operating correctly and providing support for users of the system.

Since testers have been involved in inspecting and checking the system at a high level of detail, the testers are equipped to provide information for users that may be using the system for the first time.

AGILE PROJECT WORK PRODUCTS

After completing this topic, you should be able to describe the project work products that are important to agile testers.

In this section, we'll be talking about some of the work products that are produced as part of creating and working on Agile projects.

These work products can be split into a number of different categories. And we'll look at each one separately.

First of all, we'll look at some of the business-oriented work products that come out of Agile projects.

Some examples of business-oriented work products are, for example, a description of what's needed and that can be encompassed by something like a requirement specification and typically in the form of user stories.

Another type of business-oriented work product is how to use certain products that we build.

So, user documentation and user guides are a way to explain to our users how to use the software products that we build.

Some of the development work products are descriptions of how the system is built.

So, for example, when developers create their database entity relationship diagrams, they are providing a way...a visual way for us to see how the system is planned to be built.

Also, another work product is the actual implementation of the system, which happens by writing the actual code.

And then lastly, another development work product is the code evaluation, so any automated unit tests that the developers have created as part of developing the project.

Some of the work products that are more specific to testers and the test team are descriptions of how the system is tested.

So, any documents that show test plans and test strategies describe how we plan on testing our system.

And then the actual tests of the system, which are encompassed by manual tests as well as automated test suites.

And then finally, presentations of the test results through dashboards, for example, are another work product that the test team produces.

AGILE TEST LEVELS

After completing this topic, you should be able to describe the test levels in the context of agile testing.

In this section, we'll talk about the different test levels that we may complete when achieving the Definition of Done in agile projects.

In agile projects, reaching the state where we consider a user story or a sprint to be done requires that we've defined what levels of testing we have gone through in order to achieve that state of done.

There are a number of different levels of testing that we may achieve in getting to the Definition of Done including unit testing.

So, when we say that we've completed unit testing and we're done, this can mean that we've completed all test coverage with reviews.

So, our code has been completely covered with unit testing, and we've done reviews on the unit tests internally with the development team.

It includes and it also means that an analysis of the code has been done through peer reviews or code reviews.

Any defects have been identified and fixed, if applicable. And unit tests have been code reviewed, checked in, and fully automated.

If we say that we're at the integration testing level within our achieving of Definition of Done, that means that any defects have been reported and documented when integrating the code together.

That means that we have automated regression tests, and that means that we've tested all of our acceptance criteria including positive acceptance criteria as well as negative acceptance criteria.

It also means that we've identified any quality risks after integrating the code together.

If we're at the system testing level within agile projects, that means that all of the stories in a release have been fully tested or tested end-to-end.

It means that we've tested in a staging environment or in a production-like environment.

And it means that any quality risks have been highlighted and accepted by the product's owner.

And finally, it means that we have automated regression testing that's been completed on the whole build.

These levels help us define whether we're done with our user stories, and sprint, and ultimately our projects that we're delivering in an agile environment.

AGILE TESTING AND CONFIGURATION MANAGEMENT

After completing this topic, you should be able to describe testing and test configuration management in the context of agile projects.

In this section, we'll talk about the role of configuration management for automated testing in agile environments.

Configuration management tools are tools used in agile environments or in any project environment where the tool checks in the source code and the unit tests, and then compiles and builds the code with test frameworks.

These tools usually then run a suite of automated tests.

Some of the tools that help do configuration management are Ant, JSHint, Subversion, Checkstyle, and others.

Using configuration management tools and build scripts in the context of agile projects allows for customization of the configuration as needed.

So, for example, if we need to configure certain tests to run at certain intervals for our project, we can do that with these tools.

Having an automated build process also allows different types of test suites to be run when appropriate. So potentially, we run functional tests at certain intervals and integration tests at other intervals.

[Heading: Agile Testing and Configuration Management. Some of the other tools that help do configuration management are FindBug, Jacoco, and PMD.]

Using automated tests, we're able to check the stabilization of the code, avoid delays and build failures by immediately getting feedback on the status of our integrations and our builds.

Types of builds that can be done with configuration management tools are fast builds, and these are triggered.

So, these compile and build source code changes and let us know when a complication has been detected.

A full build is typically scheduled once or twice a day and will do a build of the whole software.

This type of build isn't triggered or is not a manual build that's done for a very small subset of the code; rather it builds the whole entire code base.

And finally, push-to-QA builds are scheduled on demand, and these are builds that go through a formal QA team and will be tested by the QA team.

Configuration management tools are great tools for helping us automate the test process and run automated test suites.

AGILE AND INDEPENDENT TESTING

After completing this topic, you should be able to outline options for using independent testers on agile projects.

In this section, we'll be discussing the concept of independent test teams in agile projects.

An independent test team runs in parallel with the whole team approach but does not get integrated into the whole team.

Their main function and focus is on doing independent testing of the work products that the team is producing.

An independent test team may focus on different types of testing.

Then the team would be focusing on including investigative testing, so testing of nonfunctional requirements like performance; production readiness testing, so ensuring that the build or release is actually ready for production; and difficult types of testing that the team may not have the skill set to perform.

There are a few different scenarios when we might want to consider integrating an independent test team on our projects, such as if we work in a highly regulated environment where there is compliance that requires us by law to have our code tested independently, that's a very good reason to have an independent test team come and test our code.

Also, if we've outsourced the development of our projects, we may also want an independent test team that validates the work products of that outsourced team.

If we're working in complex domains or with complex technical environments, an independent test team may have the additional skill set and expertise to test some of our code in our software.

And then finally, when we have large or geographically distributed teams, the whole team approach can get complicated, and it's helpful to have an independent test team that can come in and test the integrated software.

Independent test teams typically support multiple project teams, which helps minimize the number of testing tool licenses that we need for the whole team.

It also helps minimize expenses for having separate independent test teams for each project. And it creates the concept of having testing specialists that are really specialized in testing across the organization.

Some of the considerations regarding independent test teams and independent testing are that agile independent test teams work differently than traditional independent test teams.

So, they have a very specific focus area, and they are not coming in at the end of a project to test all of the functional requirements and all of the requirements at the very last phase of a project.

The focus is usually on specific things like production readiness as we've mentioned or complex domains or regulatory compliance.

COMMUNICATING TEST STATUS AND PRODUCT QUALITY

After completing this topic, you should be able to describe how test status, progress, and product quality can be communicated in an agile project.

In this section, we'll be talking about some different tools and techniques for communicating test status and product quality in agile projects.

In agile projects, we have a number of different tools and techniques that we can use to record iteration status.

Some of these are the daily stand-up meetings, the sprint burndown chart, a visible task board, and correspondence including e-mail.

We will talk about a couple of these.

The sprint burndown chart is a way for us to check progress across all iterations.

Within a sprint, we don't only want to focus on what was accomplished and what is remaining, but we can also use the sprint burndown chart to measure and check certain scope changes within the course of a sprint.

Generally and ideally, we like to keep the scope of a sprint in an agile project fixed so that we have a higher probability of delivering on the user stories that we committed to at the beginning of a sprint.

However, in some cases, team members need to add scope to the project or to the sprint after getting into some of the user stories and understanding them better.

The sprint burndown chart allows us to see where things may have spiked and increased in estimates or increase some of our initial scope based on certain circumstances or certain events happening during the course of a sprint.

[Communicating Test Status and Product Quality. A sample Sprint Burndown chart is displayed. The chart includes Day in the x-axis and Remaining Effort in the y-axis. The remaining effort is plotted against the ideal effort. The chart shows the deviation of the remaining effort with the ideal effort.]

Another way to communicate status and product quality is the task board.

The task board provides a visual representation for the development and testing teams.

And it is typically split up into To Do, In Progress, and Complete columns.

Each one of these columns shows us what items and how many items are still in progress, how many of the items we still have to complete, and how many items we've completed during the course of a sprint.

Having a visual task board and a visual representation of the work allows a team to see where there may be bottlenecks and where people may need help collaborating in order to get things completed.

The daily stand-up meeting is a regularly scheduled meeting that happens every day.

The purpose of the meeting is to show what tasks will be worked on for the day, what tasks have been completed, and to discuss any impediments or blocking issues that the team has.

We like to keep these meetings short and simple, and we timebox them usually within 15 minutes.

Any conversations that need to happen that are longer than the 15 minutes can be scheduled for after the daily stand-up meeting.

Again, in this meeting, we discuss what has been done, what will be worked on today, and any impediments or blocking issues that people can either help each other with or discuss at a later time.

[Communicating Test Status and Product Quality. The daily stand-up meeting is effective in single project teams.]

MANAGING RISK REGRESSION

After completing this topic, you should be able to describe how risk regression in agile development can be managed using evolving manual and automated test cases.

In this section, we're going to be talking about regression testing and using regression testing in order to manage risk in our projects.

Regression testing is a practice where we ensure that changes and modifications in our code haven't broken existing functionality.

Regression testing is very important to help us catch bugs that may have accidentally been introduced by doing new builds, and most importantly, when we're creating release candidate builds that we want to release to production.

Regression testing also helps us ensure that bugs that may have been eradicated in previous cycles have remained eliminated and that they didn't crop up again in our new cycles.

We also want to ensure that new changes haven't resulted in a regression, so components that formerly worked aren't now failing with the new code integration.

Although automation of test suites is a great way to ensure that we're doing a lot of code coverage with our tests and we're covering a lot of scope and functionality, it's not a surefire solution when it comes to regression testing.

Some automated test suites may have some oversight when it

comes to looking into all of the different cases.

And how do we test things that used to work but now may be broken?

With regression testing, we really want to have a combination of automated test suites as well as manual testing to ensure that things are working properly, and that new code hasn't managed to break old code that used to work.

SKILLS OF AN AGILE TESTER

After completing this topic, you should be able to describe the skills that an agile tester should have.

In this section, we'll talk about the characteristics that contribute to being a really good tester in an agile environment.

In agile teams and agile projects, an agile tester must be able to be cross-functional. That means they can start to take on skill sets from the other team members.

It's ideal if agile testers are part of one single team versus trying to divide up their time amongst a number of teams.

By being part of a single team, they're able to gain domain expertise and knowledge and pick up skills from their team members.

By being a cross-functional team member, they also have the ability to build certain work items end-to-end.

And they are accountable for the outcome of the project and the product just as any other development team member would be.

Agile testers must be able to be collaborative and work well with others including the product owner and the scrum master.

Agile testers should also be organized and understand the concept of self-organizing teams and have the ability to make their own autonomous decisions.

Agile testers should feel empowered to make operational and technical decisions when it comes to their domain of expertise.

Also, agile testers should be transparent and should be willing to display their status and their tasks on the agile task board along with the other team members.

Agile testers should be committed to a certain level of product quality.

Although their aim is to satisfy the product owner and customer needs, the agile tester is really the gatekeeper for the quality of the product.

Development team members may incorporate certain activities to ensure quality in terms of their code.

However, the agile tester is really looking at quality at an overall high level and should be the last resort when it comes to ensuring quality for the team. Agile testers should also be credible.

So, they gain the trust of the team, and they also trust the team members.

Agile testers are also accountable for the work product that they produce and have integrity in reporting status.

Agile testers should also be open to feedback, which includes informal feedback.

An agile team's informal feedback is an important tool for continuous improvement.

And then finally, agile testers should be resilient and respond well to change.

Agile environments have constant change in order to maximize business value, and as we learn more about the project and the product, there will be things that change along the way.

Testers that have difficulty responding to change would have difficulty in an agile environment.

So, with agile testers, we want testers that are flexible and are able to respond well to change.

ROLE OF AN AGILE TESTER

After completing this topic, you should be able to describe the role of a tester in an agile team.

In this section, we'll talk about the role of testers in an agile environment and on agile project teams.

In an agile environment, the role of testers goes beyond simply testing software, and finding bugs, and logging defects.

The agile tester works as an integral part of the development team and is working day in and day out consistently with the development team.

The agile tester also works closely with the product owner to ensure that they really understand their requirements and what their expectations are.

And then by understanding those requirements, the tester is actually helping to improve and build a quality product by making sure that the developer's work is actually fulfilling the requirement, but also meeting the expectations of the product owner and the customer for which we're building product.

One of the important characteristics of a good agile tester is that they are really good at communication.

Part of that is attending the right meetings but also being a very effective conveyer of information.

Agile testers need to know and understand that face-to-face communication is the most effective form of communication, especially on agile teams and in agile projects.

As such, they proactively engage the right people at the right time to make sure that the right information is getting from one area of the project to another.

In addition to face-to-face communication, agile testers must also be able to communicate well through other methods, whether it's documents that show test status or e-mail, et cetera.

The agile tester also has some level of technical capability in order to provide technical input into code reviews, and some of the coding, and also some level of automation skill.

Some programming skills are required in order to be able to automate test suites and automate their test scripts so that we have a fully automated test suite and test scripts for the testers to work.

So, having automation, technical, communication skills, and being an integral part of the development team make it so that agile testers go beyond just testing software, logging bugs, and reporting defects.

THE AGILE SOFTWARE TESTING – METHODOLOGIES AND TESTING APPROACHES IS THE FIRST PART OF THE AGILE SOFTWARE TESTING COURSE.

Agile software development lifecycles are comprised of short iterations with working software released at the end of each iteration.

In this section, you will have overview of agile development and cover some of the different approaches, including Extreme Programming, Scrum, and Kanban.

You will learn the key aspects of testing in an agile environment, as well as the skillset that an agile tester should have.

- *Agile Software Development Fundamentals*: Agile Software Development and the Agile Manifesto, The Twelve Principles of the Agile Manifesto, The Whole Team Approach, Early and Frequent Feedback;

- *Aspects of Agile Approaches*: Extreme Programming (XP), Scrum, Kanban, Collaborative User Stories, Creation of User Stories, Retrospectives, Continuous Integration, Release and Iteration Planning;

- *Testing in Agile Approaches*: Agile Testing and Development Activities, Agile Project Work Products, Agile Test Levels, Agile Testing and Configuration Management, Agile and Independent Testing;

- *Test Status in Agile Projects*: Communicating Test Status and Product Quality, Managing Risk Regression;

- *Role and Skills of an Agile Tester*: Skills of an Agile Tester, Role of an Agile Tester.

TECHNIQUES AND TOOLS

The Agile Software Testing – Techniques and Tools is the second part of the Agile Software course.

Agile approaches include the complementary techniques of test-driven development, acceptance test- driven development, and behavior-driven development.

In this section, we will explore the key features of agile testing and how techniques such as black box testing can be applied in agile projects.

We will also take a look at various tools that are available to agile testers, everything from task management and tracking tools, to communication and configuration tools.

- *Agile Testing and Risk Assessment*: Test-driven and Behavior-driven Development, Test Levels, A Scrum Tester, Quality Risks in Agile Projects;

- *Techniques in Agile Projects*: Estimation of Testing Effort, Test Basis in Agile Projects, Definition of Done, Acceptance Test-driven Development, Functional and Nonfunctional Black Box Test Design, Exploratory Testing;

- *Tools for Testing in Agile Projects*: Task Management and Tracking Tools, Communication and Information-sharing Tools, Test Development and Configuration Tools.

TEST-DRIVEN AND BEHAVIOR-DRIVEN DEVELOPMENT

After completing this topic, you should be able to describe the complimentary techniques of test-driven development or TDD, acceptance test-driven development, and behavior-driven development used in agile projects.

In this section, we'll be talking about two approaches to development that make testing a core part of their approach, test-driven and behavior-driven development.

Test-driven development is a style of programming that is, just as its name implies, driven by the testing aspect.

So, initially, we're going to start by thinking about, "What tests do I need to write assuming that my code is going to fulfill all the requirements?"

The activities involved in test-driven development are, we start by writing a single unit test for the function we're about to build.

Next we're going to run the test. Obviously, since we haven't written any code yet, that test is going to fail. Next we are going to write code to pass the test.

We're going to run the tests again and then continuously refactor our code as we go through this cycle over and over again until our code is passing all of the tests and until the code is optimized.

Test-driven development is an approach where we think about,

"How can I fulfill requirements before jumping into writing code?"

Some of the potential pitfalls around test-driven development are too many tests being written at once.

So, if we try to think about all of the functionality we're trying to build and write all of the tests that we can think of all at the same time, we may be writing too many tests and trying to approach and solve too many problems at the same time.

It's best to focus on one function that you're trying to build at a time, write a single test first for it, and then make that test pass, and then write the next test, et cetera.

Another potential pitfall is writing tests that are too large and then try to test too many pieces and subsets of functionality.

Another potential pitfall is writing tests that are too trivial and too easy to make the test succeed by writing very simple code.

These tests aren't really going to get at the meat of what we're trying to solve or fulfill in terms of requirements.

Another pitfall is more cultural, and it's only partial adoption of the test-driven development approach by teams.

When we have partial adoption, then we have some level of disconnect amongst the team members when they have different approaches.

Another potential pitfall is poor maintenance of the code.

So, for writing tests that are sometimes failing and then sometimes succeeding and we don't go back and refactor our code, then we're not going to have very clean code across the board.

We need to make sure that we're refactoring and cleaning up our code and maintaining the code.

And then finally, when we have seldom used test suites, so sometimes we may write tests for our code and then not actually use them in the automated test suite process later on.

Those tests should either be verified for elimination, whether do we actually need those tests anymore, or we may go on and actually optimize them or write them in a way that then ensures that we use them moving forward.

Next we want to talk about behavior-driven development.

Behavior-driven development really stems from TDD, but also it extends it and augments it.

The following practices are some of the practices that augment TDD.

So, in behavior-driven development, we apply the Five Whys principle, which is a powerful approach at getting at the root cause of an issue or a question.

So, we'll start by asking, you know, "Why is it that that we need to fulfill this requirement?", "Why do we need to it this way?", et cetera, et cetera, and getting at the root cause of what it is actually that we're trying to fulfill.

By having outside-in thinking, we're thinking about the words really being just a representation of the behaviors that we're trying to fulfill.

So, when we're thinking from that outside-in, we're looking at, "What are the behaviors really that we're trying to fulfill through our code?" or "What are the behaviors that we're trying to enable our users?"

And then finally, describing behaviors in a single notation makes it clear to anybody who is looking at either the tests, the acceptance tests, or even the stories what it is that we're trying to do.

So, we're really writing user stories in a very common format across the board, and then we're writing acceptance tests also in a common language.

By having a common language and a common approach for how we write these things, it becomes easier for everyone across the board to understand what it is we're trying to achieve.

So, for example, in behavior-driven development, it's common to have unit test names, the whole sentences that start with a conditional verb like should.

And they should be written in order of business value.

Also, acceptance tests should be written in behavior-driven development using the standard agile framework of a user story.

So, as a specific role...so this type of user, for example, I want...and then a feature, what is the feature that I want...so that...and then you're going to explain what the benefit is.

The acceptance criteria should then be written in terms of scenarios and implemented as classes in the code.

So, given some initial context when some event occurs, then we must ensure some specific outcome.

This helps improve communication and make sure that everybody understands what it is that we're getting at.

The benefits of behavior-driven development are having improved guidance for the developers and the testers, as well as even the business team that's putting together the requirements.

It also helps us understand the intention behind the code versus thinking purely technically about implementing.

Some of the pitfalls are that it's a very conceptual approach and can be confusing in the beginning to developers who are used to thinking about technically solving the problems.

It requires familiarity with the user story language and the way that we write user stories and think about them.

However, usually once teams are familiar with this approach, it becomes a lot easier over time.

TEST LEVELS

After completing this topic, you should be able to describe the test pyramids, testing quadrants, test levels, and testing types in the context of agile projects.

In this section we're going to be explaining the concept of test levels and what test pyramids represent, and we'll talk about what the testing quadrants are in an agile environment.

As you can see, the test pyramid is a representation of the different layers of testing.

At the bottommost level, we have robust unit tests, which constitute the lower layer and are really the foundation upon which a really solid testing is built.

The next layer is having automated tests, and this is at the middle layer, and it tests the service.

And it really looks at the integration of our different pieces of code across the whole software.

And then the top layer is where we get sometimes the lowest return on investment in our testing, which is really just the user interface testing.

When you think about the functionality of the software, most of the testing and most of the bang for your buck is going to be coming from testing things at the unit level, so at the very, very lowest level of the code, and then testing at the integration level or the service level once you've integrated pieces of code together.

And then finally, the UI ensures that things are working visually the way that we expect.

We also have a concept called the testing quadrants.

And the testing quadrants represent a way to organize tests based on whether they're business facing or technology facing.

The quadrants are labeled Q1 through Q4, and they represent a number of different types of tests.

So, in quadrant 1, this is the quadrant that's really most kind of technology facing but also helps support the team.

So, these types of tests are unit tests and component tests, and they are at the lowest level of the code. Quadrant 2 is looking more at functional tests.

So, here is where we'll be testing at the user story level and ensuring that the code really fulfills the requirements of a specific user story.

And then quadrant 3 starts to get into even more business facing where we're doing exploratory testing.

So how is the usability of our code? Are things easy to use? Is the flow really intuitive?

And it also gets into user acceptance testing, so testing that we are meeting the acceptance criteria of the overall code and software.

And then quadrant 4 is again another type of technology-facing test, but it's more around performance, and load testing, and security testing, so testing how our software would behave once we release it out into production.

The different test levels that we have in agile environments are unit testing.

And if you have coverage at the unit testing level, then you really have a lot of test coverage with code reviews from the development team, and you're mainly focused on testing the units or these very smaller units of code.

Integration testing...so if you are at the integration testing level, then we're getting into more regression tests or testing the way that the software components interact together, and we're making sure that we didn't break anything.

At the system testing level, we're really testing stories in a release.

And we're ensuring that we've done end-to-end testing on how the stories in a full release are interacting and behaving, and whether we're fulfilling the business value of that release.

A SCRUM TESTER

After completing this topic, you should be able to describe the role of an agile tester within the specific context of a Scrum life cycle.

In this section, we'll talk about the role of a tester in a Scrum environment, which is a specific implementation of an Agile framework. Just as a recap, in Scrum, there is a role called the Scrum master who is really the facilitator of the product development team.

The Scrum master helps manage the process of how information is exchanged between team members as well as really facilitating a lot of the activities and ensuring that people are keeping to the process. Mainly, the Scrum master's role is to ensure that impediments that are blocking the team from making progress are removed.

Testers work closely with the Scrum masters and a Scrum team to ensure that their role is being helpful and productive and that they are contributing to development of a high-quality product.

In Scrum, the product development team has daily stand-up meetings. In those meetings, the team members collaborate, share, and communicate and basically the meeting is focused around three specific questions.

The first question being what did you work on yesterday? The second is what will you work on today? And finally, what blocking issues or impediments do you have? Testers in an Agile environment and in a Scrum environment specifically must also be asking and answering those questions for themselves and for the work that they are contributing to the team.

They are involved in the daily stand-up meetings just as the rest of the team including the development team members. And they should be updating on the status of their work as well.

The daily stand-up meeting is a great opportunity to find out what development team members could use some help in terms of thinking of different test cases or working to ensure that acceptance criteria is being met.

Some considerations for a tester in a Scrum environment are interaction is critical. So testers should be working with everybody and interacting with everybody on the team.

Testing is no longer an isolated event that happens away from the development team, where bugs and issues are reported back.

And on the contrary, the testers working alongside the team members, testing as they are developing and checking out the latest versions of the code to ensure that everything is working as expected.

Communication is also a key, so testers should be making suggestions around what things the developers might want to take into consideration as they are developing, as well as provide feedback on some of the implementation.

In addition, testers should be identifying risks with the software or with the implementation that the developers are planning and they should have some technical acumen and ability just to ensure that the appropriate technologies are being implemented and the appropriate approach is being taken.

Responsibilities of a Scrum tester and a Scrum team are that they contribute to meetings, all of the meetings including the planning meetings, the review, the sprint review meeting and the retrospective. In the planning meetings, they are thinking about the implementation of the software and the user stories and they are thinking about acceptance criteria.

They are also thinking about whether or not a certain amount of work is realistic to take on within an iteration. In the review meetings, they are part of the team just like everybody else and they are explaining what has been implemented and what has not been implemented and talking about what challenges they may have had during the sprint.

And then finally, in the retrospective, just like any other member of the team, they are providing feedback on how things went during the sprint and potential suggestions for how to improve. Scrum testers or testers in a Scrum team are also going to be writing and updating acceptance criteria, so that they make sense and performing exploratory testing.

So in addition to testing the simple straight-forward functionality of user stories, they are looking to identify whether there are any performance related bugs or any other bugs that the team might not have thought about.

QUALITY RISKS IN AGILE PROJECTS

After completing this topic, you should be able to describe how quality risk analysis takes place in agile projects.

In this section, we're going to be talking about how we assess and analyze quality risks in Agile projects and how we go about mitigating them.

The definition of a risk is any uncertainty that could positively or negatively affect the outcome of our project.

We tend to think of risks as being negative events.

However, risks can also represent opportunities for our product that we didn't think about when we first started.

So, risks are threats or opportunities that can affect the outcome of our project.

Negative risks are anything that is considered anti-value, meaning it takes away from the value of the outcome of our product or it minimizes from the value that we were delivering with our product.

That could be due to any type of technical issues or anything that takes away from our cost equations.

So maybe we're having to pay additional cost and therefore reducing our amount of profit margin or anything really that minimizes the business value to the customer.

There are multiple occasions in Agile projects when we look at and assess quality risks.

Some of those include the release planning meeting.

So at the release planning level, the product owner is going to be explaining the risk at a high level to the team and then the team will be assessing the risk and looking into more of the technical details, and the implementation, and how to get around that risk or maybe provide some more workarounds.

So, the product owner along with the rest of the team is responsible to identify and call out risks at a high-level and then work with the team to assess and go into more detail.

At the iteration planning level, the whole team is going to be reviewing every single user story for a quality risk within that user story.

Some examples of some risks that may reduce the quality of our software could be to having no test data, or having incorrect test data, or if we have slow systems, so systems that are slow to respond to the user's input data, or when we have screens that have no boundary conditions or no business logic.

So, these are some of the types of things that people will be looking at when we're assessing quality risks. Let's talk about how this is done.

So an example for a quality risk analysis process is we might call a meeting that involves the testers and all the team members.

We'll have the backlog items displayed on a task board or on a white board.

And then we'll start to go through one by one the backlog items and identify certain quality risk in each item.

Once we've identified what quality risks there are, so let's say, there is a user story that doesn't have any access to test data or insufficient test data, we'll start to categorize the level of risk and then impact that that issue poses for our project.

So is it really critical that this user story has some test data or is it not so critical, and then what is the impact of if we don't test it or if we test it incorrectly or insufficiently?

Based on that categorization, we'll then plan the testing efforts based on the level of risk.

So we want to look at things that have a high level of risk and maybe potentially put those at the top of our lists, and test those, so that we're assured that we're looking at things with the high level of risks first to give the team time to address those issues.

And then we want to select the appropriate technique to mitigate the risk.

So, is it something that we can mitigate through a workaround or do we need to have a very different technical implementation of the whole user story?

So, these are the ways that we look at quality risks, assess them, and then potentially analyze how we can go around working around them and mitigating the risks.

ESTIMATION OF TESTING EFFORT

After completing this topic, you should be able to describe how to estimate testing effort in an agile project based on content and risk.

In this section, we're going to be talking about how we estimate testing effort in an Agile project.

In Agile projects, testers are working closely with the development team and they are working hand-in-hand to collaborate and work together through the course of an iteration.

As such, estimation is really based off of those user stories that the development team is implementing.

So, the whole team is looking together at the priority level, complexity level, and the overall effort required to both, implement the tests and then release those user stories to production.

So also, since the testers are working in conjunction with the development team, estimation is something that they are going to be doing on an ongoing basis.

It's an ongoing activity, where testers are constantly looking and monitoring any obstacles that the development team is having, any issues that they are having in completing their tasks, as well as looking at any tasks that are getting finished on time or ahead of schedule.

So it's really going to be important for Agile testers on an Agile team to know what is the development team members' progress and what is their status with different user stories and tasks, so that the testers are on top of it and they are ready to test whatever is coming their way based on knowing what's happening with the development team.

So unit testing is something that is going to be done on an Agile team, where there are tests that test each unit of software separately.

And doing unit testing on an Agile team really requires collaborative estimation with the whole team.

So, the testers are going to involve the development team to say, with these unit tests what's the level of effort required to test these components that you are developing.

With test-driven developments, there are some activities that are involved that are really more developer centric.

So the developers themselves are doing the coding and testing of design of their units of software.

Test-driven development means building unit tests to tests those units of software, but also there can be automated tests suites that include unit tests that the testers can then run in order to ensure that things are still working as planned and especially in a regression scenario where they're testing that new code has not broken code that's already been written.

So some opportunities where we're doing estimations of testing effort and overall effort are during some of the planning meetings.

So within a sprint, we have the sprint planning meeting, which forces really the team to think about what the efforts required are to implement the user stories.

And when we're talking about effort required, we're thinking about the development and everything that's involved in the development including the testing as a piece of that.

Looking in the planning meetings at those effort estimates is going to help us really understand the overall product estimates for the release and for the entire product.

Coming up with estimates is really a collaborative process that involves brainstorming at the whole team level and then collaborating to make sure that acceptance tests and acceptance criteria are really covering all of the cases and scenarios that we need to cover, and then asking questions to ensure that we understand what has been requested, and then finally, reviewing both doing the code reviews as well as reviewing the tests to ensure that our testing is exhaustive and it covers what we need to cover.

TEST BASIS IN AGILE PROJECTS

After completing this topic, you should be able to describe the types of test bases, including user stories, that are available to agile testers.

In this section, we'll talk about how we create a basis for our testing efforts in Agile projects.

So test analysis in Agile projects is a process where we want to review something for the purpose of coming up with test information.

Before we do our testing analysis, we need to come up with a test basis.

The test basis is the information that we need in order to even start doing our test analysis.

And that information is encompassed in the requirements, specifications, risk analysis, and the architecture for our project.

So we're going to look at our user stories, we're going to look at any technical specifications that we have, and any of the risk analysis that we've done for the projects, as well as the architecture that we know we're building our software on. Once we have that information, then we can start doing our test analysis.

Test conditions are things that we need to come up with as part of doing our test analysis to come up with different cases that we know are going to be testing.

So a condition in the testing jargon is something that can be tested.

For example, one of the conditions may be what happens if we have a 0 as a value or what happens if I put a letter instead of a number.

We want to identify as many conditions as possible for the purposes of what we're trying to test.

And then we're going to select a number of those conditions and combine them to create test cases.

So the test conditions that we're going to be worried about or that we're going to be concerned with in terms of planning our testing depend on our test strategy.

And that strategy might be to test everything, it might be to test very specific cases, it might be to test only the case that we know is going to happen 99% of the time.

We have to come up with a test strategy first to know what it is we're looking for before we can understand what conditions we are going to be concerned with.

And then test conditions can be identified for test data, test inputs, as well as the test outcomes.

When we're looking at possible tests, we need to understand that we can't always test everything.

So testing everything is referred to as exhaustive testing.

An exhaustive testing is not typically very realistic in the context of doing testing for a project. Instead, we're going to be doing a subset of everything.

We're going to look at what subsets of the tests are going to help us find the most number of defects.

So our test technique is going to be the process of selecting that subset that's going to encompass a majority of our cases and it's going to help us find the majority of the defects in our code.

DEFINITION OF DONE

After completing this topic, you should be able to outline the import-
ance of the Definition of Done in test levels and in different stages in
the agile process.

In this section, we'll be exploring the concept of Definition of
Done and how it's applied in Agile projects.

In Agile projects, Agile teams typically have something they call
the Definition of Done to ensure that what they are working on is
potentially shippable.

So the Definition of Done is a clear and concise list of requirements that if fulfilled means that our code or our software is now
potentially shippable.

Definition of Done in that list of requirements should be a live
document that's reviewed regularly by the team to ensure rele-
vance and to make sure that that list makes sense for what we're
working on at the moment.

The product owner is responsible for ensuring that the Definition
of Done has been documented and then the team is accountable
for fulfilling that list of requirements to ensure that their code is
shippable.

The Definition of Done ensures that we have a list of criteria that's
accepted by the product owner and that we have an agreed and
shared understanding when we're going to consider things ready
for release.

We can create a Definition of Done at various levels in our projects.

So we can have different definitions of done for a feature, a sprint, and a release.

Typically, the things that we need to consider as criteria for something to be done at a feature level are going to be different than that at a sprint level and a release level.

So in order for a story or a product backlog item to be considered done, we might have a certain sort of criteria that's different than for the collection of features once they're integrated into a sprint, that's then different than those criteria for considering a release to be potentially shippable.

The benefits of having a clear and concise list of criteria to consider something done is that it guides the pre-implementation activities that we do as a team.

So it guides our discussion, it guides our estimation efforts, and it guides the design of the software once we know what types of things we need to have fulfilled in order to be potentially shippable.

It also limits costs of rework, for example, by having us understand upfront what things are expected in order to consider our software done.

So, developers won't have come to the end of a sprint and then realize that their code isn't actually potentially shippable because of some criteria that hasn't been discussed or documented in Definition of Done.

Having a Definition of Done also helps to limit misunderstandings and conflict that could arise between the team members or the team members and the product owner by not having a clear and communicated list of criteria from the very beginning.

Some of the potential pitfalls on focusing on Definition of Done is that there...it could be counter-productive to focus too much on having a list of criteria versus just doing the work.

Sometimes some teams may spend too much time coming up

with the list of what is considered done and focus a little bit less on actually implementing or getting to the work.

Also individual features and user stories may require some additional general work that's not encompassed by the Definition of Done for every single case.

However, having done via shared understanding may also lose effectiveness over time if we're not constantly reviewing, and revising, and ensuring that our Definition of Done is relevant and kept up to date.

ACCEPTANCE TEST-DRIVEN DEVELOPMENT

After completing this topic, you should be able to describe how acceptance test-driven development is applied in agile projects.

In this section, we'll be talking about acceptance test-driven development, what it means, it's implications on your Agile project and some tools that can help you implement it.

Acceptance test-driven development is a collaborative practice.

In acceptance test-driven development, application developers, software users, and then business analysts come together and collaborate to come up with some acceptance criteria upfront in the project.

They then work on automating those acceptance criteria and then having those automated acceptance criteria really drive the development phase.

So ATDD really focuses on communication, collaboration, and providing clarity to app developers upfront and early in the project.

So in ATDD, acceptance tests are a set of tests that must pass before the software is considered finished.

Traditionally, testers run acceptance tests at the end of the software development phase.

ATDD takes a different approach. So ATDD involves, as we said before, collaboratively defining, then automating the acceptance tests for an upcoming project before starting the development phase and helps ensure all project members understand what needs to be done up front.

And then the difference with ATDD is that after automating the tests, instead of being run independently at the end of the development phase, they run throughout the project.

They also help the developers to find what they need to write in terms of software to fulfill and to pass those acceptance tests.

So ATDD tests are derived from acceptance criteria. In many of our setions, we've talked about using user stories as a way to define requirements for Agile projects.

User stories typically come with a set of acceptance criteria.

We use those acceptance criteria to define the automated tests and the acceptance tests that we're going to use for ATDD.

It's important to know that ATDD tests are not an exhaustive list of all the technical testing that needs to happen on the software that the developers are developing, rather it's more a validation of requirements and of the acceptance criteria and making sure that we're meeting requirements from a business perspective.

Again, ATDD is focused on automating these acceptance tests.

And this is important because the objective is to have living executable tests that are executed automatically when any changes are made to the source code.

This provides objective measurement of progress since, as we know in Agile, the most important measurement of progress is having software that runs, and succeeds, and passes our tests.

Having to write acceptance tests upfront also helps the developers have a heads up in terms of what the complexity is going to be for their software that they need to write.

If, for example, writing certain acceptance tests is going to be difficult and complex, then that probably gives us a sense that the feature or the story that we're also trying to implement is going to be difficult or complex when we come to writing the software.

There are a number of tools that are really helpful if your team is implementing ATDD.

Some of those tools are FitNesse, which is a simple tool. It's not very technical and it helps us run a suite of automated acceptance tests.

Another tool is Concordion, which provides an acceptance testing framework. It's expressed in the form of HTML pages and contains free-form text and tables and allows people to define what the framework they want in order to run through a number of tests with every release, or iteration, or throughout the development phase.

Finally, we'll note that while some of these tools are really helpful in implementing ATDD, ATDD is really more of a mindset for your team.

And the tool that you select should just be the one that makes more sense for your team and integrates well with your development team's environment.

FUNCTIONAL AND NONFUNCTIONAL BLACK BOX TEST DESIGN

After completing this topic, you should be able to describe how functional and nonfunctional black box testing techniques can be applied in agile testing.

In this section, we'll be talking about black box testing and what it means to do functional and nonfunctional black box testing in your Agile projects.

Black box testing is a software testing method that examines the functionality of an application or a method in your software.

You can apply black box testing to unit testing, integration testing, system testing, and acceptance testing, so all of the different levels of testing that you are going to run with your software testing team.

Black box testing is really intended to look at whether a certain method or a certain piece of software functions as expected.

Some of the advantages of running black box testing is that it's unbiased because it is being performed by a nontechnical team member.

The tests in black box testing are performed from the user's point of view not the designer of the software.

So, when we're running black box testing, we're running tests as a user to confirm and validate that the software is running as we expect and it's doing what we expect it to do functionally.

Some of the disadvantages of black box testing are the tests can be redundant or sometimes going to run the same type of tests over and over just to ensure functionality.

Also, designing test cases can get really complicated especially with the low-level system requirements that are more technical that might be really hard to set up for a user, for example, to test.

Some of the stuff that we develop is really what we call backend software.

And with backend software, that's really more systems related, it's a little bit harder to set up black box tests from a user perspective.

Because of that complication, many program paths can go untested because we're not going to be testing every single thing that might happen.

We're going to be testing some of the majority cases that will happen from, again, a user's perspective.

So going back to the concept of functional testing, functional testing is related to the functional requirements of a system, what functions are we expecting the system or the software to implement or make available to us?

Those go back to the business requirements.

Functional testing is performed by software testers and evaluates the systems compliance to our requirements.

Testers will verify specific actions or functions that a user needs to be able to execute in the software and then they will perform these usually manually, but also they can be automated, so you can automate a set of user tests.

Nonfunctional testing is not related to testing the specific functionality of the software.

Rather, when we perform nonfunctional testing, we're testing the nonfunctional requirements of the software.

And those relate to some of the things related to the system like the performance, scalability, usability, security, behavior, things like speed, how fast does my application respond, and how does it perform under pressure, how does it perform when we have a large load of information or data that we're sending to it.

So all of these types of things are considered nonfunctional requirements of a system.

And ideally, you've identified what are the nonfunctional requirements of your software, and thereby, the testers can test those requirements and ensure that they are also fulfilling the needs of the product owner or the customer.

EXPLORATORY TESTING

After completing this topic, you should be able to describe the import-ance of exploratory testing in agile testing.

In this section, we're going to be talking about exploratory test-ing and how you can use exploratory testing for your Agile pro-ject.

In exploratory testing, testers are simultaneously running test design, execution, and learning.

So what we mean by that is a tester hasn't really planned all of the exploratory testing upfront.

They are designing a test and then simultaneously executing it and learning more about the program.

This testing is really great for use when we're thinking about what could happen in a real life scenario when we actually release this software to production.

Exploratory testing emphasizes autonomy, skill, and creativity on the tester's part.

It's really up to the creativity of the tester to think about what things they might be able to test and how they might be able to simulate a real life scenario and come up with test cases that we might not have thought about when we were originally planning the software.

So exploratory testing goes beyond the functional requirements of the software and thinks more about special scenarios.

So as we mentioned, in exploratory testing, there are various test related activities, including designing the tests, how are we going to test this scenario...actually, executing the test, how am I going to execute this scenario that might not really be typical of what we would expect it to use.

But sometimes it makes sense and it's worth our while to actually invest some time in designing the execution of a test and a test case that might not represent the majority of what we expect to be used in the real world.

And then finally, interpreting the test results, do the test results indicate that there's something wrong with our software or is that really just a farfetched scenario that doesn't really indicate that we need to make a fix or do some changes to our software.

In exploratory testing, there is also a focus on adaptability.

We need to be able to respond to changing contexts, and try different testing techniques, and then finally, test other areas of the software.

Exploratory testing requires a mindset that's very adaptable and flexible, where the tester can go in and test certain scenarios and then try different ways of testing.

With exploratory testing, there are a number of values that go back to the original Agile Manifesto
values.

So if you think about the Agile Manifesto values, for example, valuing individuals and interactions over processes and tools that aligns really well with the concept of exploratory testing.

We're thinking about people. How would people use our software?

How would they interact with it or what are the specific tools that I'm going to use to, for example, automate my test suite?

Also, we value working software over comprehensive documentation.

So how can I look at that value and think about I want to make sure that my software really, really works.

And when we say works, we are not just talking about functionally.

We need to make sure that it's flexible, that it works in different scenarios.

And that's more important than having comprehensive documentation of all of the very specific test cases that might ever happen.

Another value is we value customer collaboration over contract negotiation.

Maybe our customer has some different scenarios or some different ideas on different scenarios that they want tested.

We want to make sure that we can accommodate all of those tests and look at those versus try to negotiate new testing scenarios in our contract.

And finally, we value responding to change over following a plan.

And that again, aligns perfectly with exploratory testing.

Because if something has changed or if the market has changed, or the environment has changed, we want to be able to come up with new test cases that can test all of those new scenarios versus following a very specific plan that we may have put in the beginning of the project.

Obviously, testing the functional requirements and following our test plan is going to be important.

But this final value also mentions that it's important to be able to respond to any changes that happen along the project.

Some considerations to think about with exploratory testing are to start with simple scenarios.

Start with things that maybe a little bit more simple easier to test. Test the nouns and the verbs of the software.

So for example, if our requirements say that our software should be able to do this certain thing or must be able to provide this other thing that we want to test the should and the must.

Then we move on to having more tools that will help us figure out our exploratory testing like the context diagrams.

Looking at those diagrams will help us figure out what are some ways that we can look at the software in a different context or in a different workflow and test those different workflows.

Look at the variables of the software, are they exhaustive? Do they fulfill all of their requirements?

Look at maybe some of the project charters and the documentation related to the project.

And then finally, look at some of the sessions that we've been running through with users, so maybe usability sessions and using those as an opportunity to do some exploratory testing.

And also reporting, it's important to report the results of exploratory testing, so that the developers can know whether or not something needs to be changed in the software and we can have a discussion on the results of those exploratory tests.

TASK MANAGEMENT AND TRACKING TOOLS

After completing this topic, you should be able to describe the types of task management and tracking tools used in agile projects and available to agile testers.

In this section, we're going to be talking about the importance of task management and tracking in your Agile project.

And we'll provide an example of a tool that can help you do so if you are not all collocated in the same location.

As we've talked about in previous sections, in Agile projects, we typically have a number of physical boards that allow us to track our progress on the project and communicate status.

So some of these are, for example, the team's task boards.

With the task boards, teams are able to manage their tasks and requirements as well as continuously prioritize stories with their product owner.

It's a very visible physical board that allows everybody to understand what exactly is going on at any given moment in the project.

We also have a number of charts like burndown and burnup charts that we can place physically in the teams working area.

They allow us to estimate our project in terms of where are we trending.

With our velocity across the number of iterations that we have with this release, are we trending along a line that means that we're going to be able to release on time or are we not?

The release planning process also gives us visibility into what we're looking for for the release and how many iterations it might take us to complete the work.

And then we also have access to a number of visual reports that we can produce that, for example, that include charts, and dashboards, and can show our progress at a very visible level.

Sometimes, if the team is not collocated, we start looking for opportunities to use an electronic tool that will still fulfill all of these things in terms of communication and collaboration across the team.

It's very important that you find a tool that works well for your team and your environment and makes people feel like they're still connected to the rest of the team and that the appropriate communication is still happening.

One example of such tool is called Planbox. We wanted to illustrate the concept of what types of things you would want to look for in an electronic tool using this specific example.

So Planbox is a software tool that teams can use to do a number of functions.

For example, they can use it to prioritize and to plan their Agile project. It helps you create a backlog and you have access to velocity charts.

In Planbox, you can also monitor progress using burndown charts and progress bars to show you where you are in your project.

With Planbox, you can also set deadline, so you can assign deadlines to items.

You can then create reminders and integrate with your calendar.

Planbox allows you to customize your set up, so you have the four-level project structure, where at the top-level, you have initiatives that then breakdown into a number of projects, and items, and then breakdown finally into tasks.

You don't have to use the concept of initiatives, for example, if you want to directly jump into using projects.

Planbox allows you to loop in your customers and get feedback and actually link some of that feedback to specific items in your backlog.

You can also have access to reports. So there are a number of standard charts and graphs that are produced.

And you can also customize and tell the tool what types of charts and graphs you also want in your reports.

So Planbox is just one example of an electronic tool that allows teams to fulfill

some of the things that they would expect to be able to do together in an Agile project, such as collaborating in real-time, sharing, working easily together, tracking their progress, having very specific to-do lists and then staying up to date with the progress of everybody else on the team.

COMMUNICATION AND INFORMATION-SHARING TOOLS

After completing this topic, you should be able to describe the types of tools used for communication and information sharing in agile teams including agile testers.

In this section, we're going to be talking about a number of different communication and information-sharing tools that people can utilize in their Agile teams.

Agile projects, it's very important to be able to communicate and share information across the different team members.

There are a number of ways that we communicate these days that can be utilized in Agile projects. For example, we're all familiar with writing e-mails in order to share information.

E-mails allow us to expedite the exchange of information, especially for distributed team members and exchange information.

They allow us to coordinate and set up times for meetings, or times to share, or times to do code reviews, et cetera, et cetera.

When we have the chance, however, verbal communication is always more powerful than written communication.

And we achieve verbal communication through daily stand-ups and regularly scheduled meetings.

Another tool that a lot of Agile teams utilize are Wikis. With

Wikis, we can plan and manage projects together.

We can share information. We have a lot of things that we can document from the conception of the project, all the way to the completion.

It's a great way to create checklists and have a one certain area for the whole team to go to when they have frequently asked questions and also to just collaborate on certain tasks.

Wikis are really flexible and they are great way for team members to collaborate, and communicate, and really customize their use of the Wiki-based on what makes the more sense for them.

Another tool that team members can use is desktop sharing.

Desktop sharing is really great for distributed teams, especially if they want to implement some practices, such as pair programming, or doing code reviews, or doing demos for each other's work, and then finally doing certain coding exercises together.

Desktop sharing also helps us capture learning experiences.

So, for doing a demo when we're doing desktop sharing, we can sometimes actually record that interaction and see where there have been issues with running through our software or where we come up with some challenges.

And it allows us to find an opportunity for continuous improvement.

When we share our desktops, we're really opening up our development environment to other developers.

And we're opening it up and making it, so that we're vulnerable in some ways to getting feedback from our team members, but that vulnerability ultimately helps us get to a level of quality with our code.

Some other tools that team members can utilize are instant messaging, actually calling people on the phone, having video chats, which allow face to face communication even for distributed team members.

And sometimes video chat can actually be low cost if we're using VoIP.

So the point of this section is to talk about the different tools that are available to team members and actually to emphasize that there is never a reason not to have face to face communication with your team members and not to have very direct two-way communication.

We have a number of technology tools available to us these days that allow for that type of collaboration and communication.

And also as we like to emphasize, face to face communication and verbal communication are always the most powerful.

TEST DEVELOPMENT AND CONFIGURATION TOOLS

After completing this topic, you should be able to outline the tools available for agile test design, development, and execution and outline the available configuration management tools, including virtualization tools for agile tests.

In this course, we're going to be talking about a number of tools that Agile team members can use for the testing, the development, and the configuration of the software.

In Agile software development projects, we have access to a number of different tools that help us in the testing, and the development, and actually the configuration of our builds and releases.

Some of these tools are more specific to developers and other tools are more specific to the testing and the quality aspects of our software.

So, for example, Sonar is a developer tool that's specific to developers and provides static analysis on their code.

It allows developers to ensure that they have good code coverage.

JUnit is another framework or a tool that is actually specific to unit testing.

So, developers or actually quality assurance engineers that have more of a developer background can create a number of unit tests that provide code coverage and then also automate the process of running those tests on the code.

There are a number of example tools that a development team in an Agile project might utilize for their project, including Ant, FindBug, Subversion.

And as you can see, from the names of these tools, some of them are more specific to the quality aspects and to finding bugs and issues with the code and others are more concerned with, for example, maintaining the latest version of our code and versioning of the software.

It's important to take a look at all of the different tools that are available to your team and ensure that ones that you select are used across your organization in a consistent way, so that they make sense for the organization and that they provide one standard way of communicating and providing feedback across the organization.

So, when we use build scripts and some of these common tools, really the objective that we want to achieve and some of the criteria that you're going to look for in these tools is that they allow for customization.

We want to be able to customize, for example, the build process.

Do we want our tool to build and release code at every checking of code or do we want to schedule that process?

We want to be able to have some level of flexibility with our tools, so that we provide the same flexibility to our customers in terms of creating new builds and releases and testing the software.

These tools have the concept of centralizing the control.

So, the tool will actually be the one central place where we centralize the build, and the release, and then the testing of the software, and potentially their reporting.

However, we have decentralized execution, which means that it should be accessible to people across the organization and anybody on the team should be able to go into the tool and, for example, run a build or ensure that the latest version of the software is checked in.

And then finally, the criteria that you want to look for in each of these tools is that it will be easily deployed on your existing infrastructure.

So, some tools allow us to automate the build of our software.

When we automate builds, we also want to run a number of functional tests at a number of different levels.

So, automating the testing can be done at the integration level as well as at the system level.

We want to run automated tests every time we integrate software, and we also want to run a number of automated tests at the higher system level of the whole software.

It's important to note that actually we have automated functional tests that run separately from our automated unit tests.

Unit tests are more of a developer type of testing and they run more frequently as developers are developing the software.

Functional tests are really run at a higher level and test the functionality of the user requirements in order to make sure that the software is fulfilling the business requirements.

Automated tests allow us to check the stability of our code and ensure that we maintain a certain level of stability across the project.

By automating the testing, we actually have access to a side of regression tests that help us avoid delay and help us avoid the failure of builds by giving us feedback on a consistent basis across the project versus only running testing at the end of the project.

Finally, it's important to note that although there are number of tools available for teams to utilize within their Agile projects, the first thing you want to do is nail down your process.

How is our team implementing Agile projects? What are the most important things that we need help or support with?

What are the most important things that matter for us in our environment for our project, for our organization, and maybe for our customers?

Once you've figured out those things, then look for tools that help support all of your objectives and your goals.

You want to look for tools that integrate well with your team and then make sense for you and your team members.

So first figure out your process and then figure out the tools that help support you in your Agile projects.

TEST DEVELOPMENT AND CONFIGURATION TOOLS

After completing this topic, you should be able to outline the tools available for agile test design, development, and execution and outline the available configuration management tools, including virtualization tools for agile tests.

In this section, we're going to be talking about a number of tools that Agile team members can use for the testing, the development, and the configuration of the software.

In Agile software development projects, we have access to a number of different tools that help us in the testing, and the development, and actually the configuration of our builds and releases.

Some of these tools are more specific to developers and other tools are more specific to the testing and the quality aspects of our software.

So, for example, Sonar is a developer tool that's specific to developers and provides static analysis on their code.

It allows developers to ensure that they have good code coverage.

JUnit is another framework or a tool that is actually specific to unit testing.

So, developers or actually quality assurance engineers that have more of a developer background can create a number of unit tests that provide code coverage and then also automate the process of running those tests on the code.

There are a number of example tools that a development team in an Agile project might utilize for their project, including Ant, FindBug, Subversion.

And as you can see, from the names of these tools, some of them are more specific to the quality aspects and to finding bugs and issues with the code and others are more concerned with, for example, maintaining the latest version of our code and versioning of the software.

It's important to take a look at all of the different tools that are available to your team and ensure that ones that you select are used across your organization in a consistent way, so that they make sense for the organization and that they provide one standard way of communicating and providing feedback across the organization.

So, when we use build scripts and some of these common tools, really the objective that we want to achieve and some of the criteria that you're going to look for in these tools is that they allow for customization.

We want to be able to customize, for example, the build process.

Do we want our tool to build and release code at every checking of code or do we want to schedule that process?

We want to be able to have some level of flexibility with our tools, so that we provide the same flexibility to our customers in terms of creating new builds and releases and testing the software.

These tools have the concept of centralizing the control.

So, the tool will actually be the one central place where we centralize the build, and the release, and then the testing of the software, and potentially their reporting.

However, we have decentralized execution, which means that it should be accessible to people across the organization and anybody on the team should be able to go into the tool and, for example, run a build or ensure that the latest version of the software is checked in.

And then finally, the criteria that you want to look for in each of these tools is that it will be easily deployed on your existing infrastructure.

So, some tools allow us to automate the build of our software.

When we automate builds, we also want to run a number of functional tests at a number of different levels.

So, automating the testing can be done at the integration level as well as at the system level.

We want to run automated tests every time we integrate software, and we also want to run a number of automated tests at the higher system level of the whole software.

It's important to note that actually we have automated functional tests that run separately from our automated unit tests.

Unit tests are more of a developer type of testing and they run more frequently as developers are developing the software.

Functional tests are really run at a higher level and test the functionality of the user requirements in order to make sure that the software is fulfilling the business requirements.

Automated tests allow us to check the stability of our code and ensure that we maintain a certain level of stability across the project.

By automating the testing, we actually have access to a side of regression tests that help us avoid delay and help us avoid the failure of builds by giving us feedback on a consistent basis across the project versus only running testing at the end of the project.

Finally, it's important to note that although there are number of tools available for teams to utilize within their Agile projects, the first thing you want to do is nail down your process.

How is our team implementing Agile projects? What are the most important things that we need help or support with?

What are the most important things that matter for us in our environment for our project, for our organization, and maybe for our customers?

Once you've figured out those things, then look for tools that help support all of your objectives and your goals.

You want to look for tools that integrate well with your team and then make sense for you and your team members.

So first figure out your process and then figure out the tools that help support you in your Agile projects.

The Agile Software Testing – Techniques and Tools is the second part of the Agile Software course.

Agile approaches include the complementary techniques of test-driven development, acceptance test- driven development, and behavior-driven development

In this section, we will explore the key features of agile testing and how techniques such as black box testing can be applied in agile projects.

We will also take a look at various tools that are available to agile testers, everything from task management and tracking tools, to communication and configuration tools.

- *Agile Testing and Risk Assessment*: Test-driven and Behavior-driven Development, Test Levels, A Scrum Tester, Quality Risks in Agile Projects;

- *Techniques in Agile Projects*: Estimation of Testing Effort, Test Basis in Agile Projects, Definition of Done, Acceptance Test-driven Development, Functional and Nonfunctional Black Box Test Design, Exploratory Testing;

- *Tools for Testing in Agile Projects*: Task Management and Tracking Tools, Communication and Information-sharing Tools, Test Development and Configuration Tools.